BOOK WORMS

OPPOSITES

Open Shut

Apple Jordan

 **Marshall Cavendish**
Benchmark
New York

The door is open.

The door is shut.

The drawer is open.

The drawer is shut.

The book is open.

The book is shut.

The window is open.

The window is shut.

My eyes are open.

My eyes are shut!

Words We Know

Door

Drawer

Book

Window

Eyes

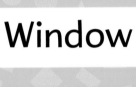

13

Index

About the Author

Apple Jordan has written many books for children, including a number of titles in the Bookworms series. She lives in upstate New York with her husband and two children. She volunteers at her local library and loves reading to kids.

With thanks to the Reading Consultants:

Nanci Vargas, Ed.D., is an Assistant Professor of Elementary Education at the University of Indianapolis.

Beth Walker Gambro is an Adjunct Profesor at the University of St. Francis in Joliet, Illinois.

Library of Congress
Cataloging-in-Publication Data

Jordan, Apple.
Open shut / Apple Jordan.
p. cm. — (Bookworms. Opposites.)
Includes index.
Summary: "Depicts familiar items that are open and items that are shut to demonstrate the concept of open and shut"—Provided by publisher.
ISBN 978-1-60870-423-1
1. English language—Synonyms and antonyms—Juvenile literature. I. Title.
PE1591.J67 2011
428.1—dc22   2010039294

Editor: Joy Bean
Publisher: Michelle Bisson
Art Director: Anahid Hamparian
Series Designer: Virginia Pope

Photo research by Tracey Engel

Cover: Jurgen Magg/Alamy (left); Getty/DK Stock/Kevin RL Hanson (right)
Title page: Nicki Pardo/Getty (left); Heide Benser/Corbis (right)

The photographs in this book are used by permission and through the courtesy of: *Superstock*:agefotostock,2,12(left). *Stock-photoPro*: didi/A.collection, 3. *Getty*: Ruth Jenkinson, 4, 12 (right); Ray Kachatorian, 6, 13 (top); Michael Hitoshi, 9; Nicki Pardo, 10, 13 (bottom). *Corbis*: William Geddes/Beateworks, 5; Heide Benser, 11. *Shutterstock*: Dmitriy Shironosov, 7; Diego Cervo, 8, 13 (middle).

Printed in Malaysia (T)
1 3 5 6 4 2